21st Century
Junior Library

INFOGRAPHICS:
STRATEGIC STATISTICS

Sports-Graphics Jr.

Stephanie Loureiro

Published in the United States of America by:

CHERRY LAKE PRESS
2395 South Huron Parkway, Suite 200, Ann Arbor, Michigan 48104
www.cherrylakepress.com

Reading Adviser: Beth Walker Gambro, MS, Ed., Reading Consultant, Yorkville, IL

Photo Credits: © OnstOn/Getty Images, © Natalia Darmoroz/Getty Images, © Aryo Hadi/Getty Images, © ginosphotos/Getty Images, © Shendart/Getty Images, cover; © Jessica Orozco, 14; © Jessica Orozco, 15; © Designer/Getty Images, © ozcan yalaz/Getty Images, 19; © ColourCreatype/Shutterstock, © matsabe/Shutterstock, 20; © ColourCreatype/Shutterstock, 21

Cherry Lake Press is an imprint of Cherry Lake Publishing Group.

Library of Congress Cataloging-in-Publication Data has been filed and is available at catalog.loc.gov.

Cherry Lake Publishing Group would like to acknowledge the work of the Partnership for 21st Century Learning, a Network of Battelle for Kids. Please visit Battelle for Kids online for more information.

Printed in the United States of America

Note from publisher: Websites change regularly, and their future contents are outside of our control. Supervise children when conducting any recommended online searches for extended learning opportunities.

ABOUT THE AUTHOR

Stephanie Loureiro is a writer and editor. She's been writing since she was nine years old and loves working on books that help kids discover things they love. When she's not writing, she can be found curled up reading a book, doing Olympic weightlifting, or singing loudly and dancing around to Taylor Swift. She currently lives in Idaho with her husband, daughter, and two dogs.

CONTENTS

STATS AND SPORTS

People keep track of their favorite teams and players. They want to know how well they are doing. That's where **statistics** and **analytics** comes in.

Statistics is a science. It is for studying **data**. Analytics is the information learned from that. Both are used for rankings.

In college basketball, for example, a team's ranking is called its "seed." The seed number is assigned by the team's season record or win percentage (games won / total games played). The seed number can tell how likely it is that a team will make it to the championship.

MARCH MADNESS: PERCENT CHANCE OF REACHING THE FINAL FOUR CHAMPIONSHIP

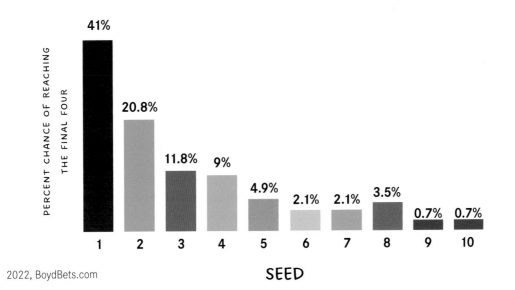

2022, BoydBets.com

ALL ABOUT THE NUMBERS

Most major sports use analytics. There is one sport that uses it the most. It is baseball! It was the first to use analytics. People use stats to make **predictions.** They guess how players will do. This gives teams a winning edge. Batting average is an example. It tells you how well a player might do when they are at bat. It is found like this:

player's total # of **hits** / player's total # of **at bats**

BASEBALL TERM:

hits: when a batter hits the ball with the bat and the ball does not go past foul lines and the batter gets on base

at bats: the number of times a player has a turn batting against the other team

AVERAGE BASEBALL STATS

Batting Average
(player's hits / player's total at bats)

Home Runs
(total number of home runs a player hits)

BA: .330

HR: 44

RBIs: 139

Runs Batted In
(total number of runs a team scores because of player's at bats)

The player who leads the **league** in these three wins the Triple Crown. And the most recent Triple Crown goes to . . . Miguel Cabrera of the Detroit Tigers!

2022, Baseball-Reference.com

HISTORY OF SPORTS ANALYTICS

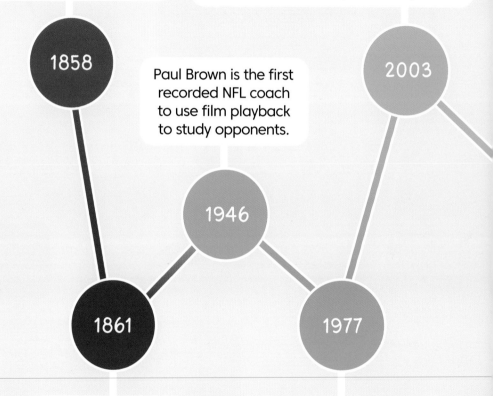

Henry Chadwick is a sportswriter. He develops a **metric** called the box score. A box score is a summary of the results of a game.

Michael Lewis's book *Moneyball* comes out. It tells the story of Billy Beane. Beane successfully used sabermetrics for the Oakland Athletics. The book drives a boom in sports analytics.

1858

Paul Brown is the first recorded NFL coach to use film playback to study opponents.

2003

1946

1861

1977

The first written sports analysis is made. It's a book called *Beadle's Dime Base-Ball Player*.

Bill James comes up with a mathematical system called sabermetrics. It **evaluates** baseball players.

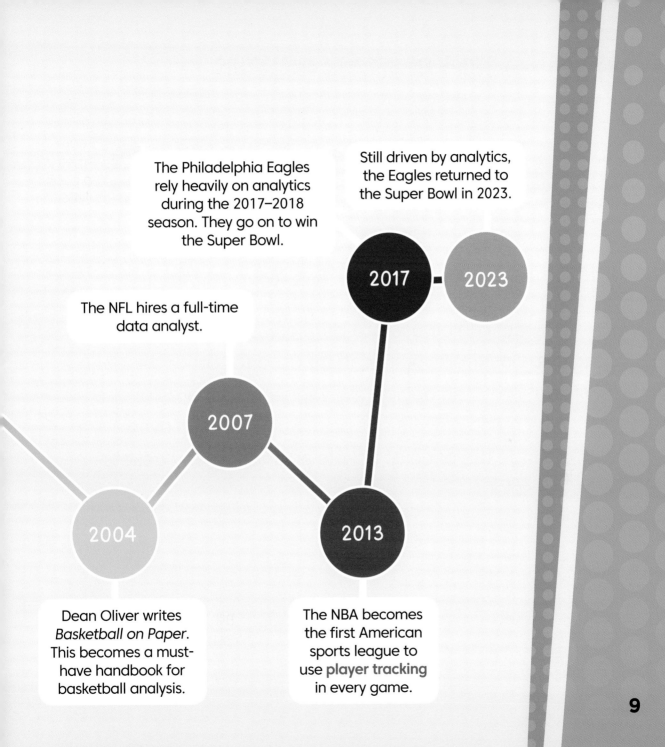

The Philadelphia Eagles rely heavily on analytics during the 2017–2018 season. They go on to win the Super Bowl.

Still driven by analytics, the Eagles returned to the Super Bowl in 2023.

2017 - 2023

The NFL hires a full-time data analyst.

2007

2004

2013

Dean Oliver writes *Basketball on Paper*. This becomes a must-have handbook for basketball analysis.

The NBA becomes the first American sports league to use **player tracking** in every game.

MONEYMAKING STATS

Stats can be used to predict how games turn out. But sports stats can be used for other things, too. They can decide the winners of awards or how much players get paid. Statistics can even change the price of tickets and how many tickets are sold.

Teams and players make money with stats. It is important for players and teams to perform well. Sales go down if they don't. Fewer ticket sales means less total money. And that means a smaller salary. **Revenue** and salary are very important. There is a whole world of stats analysis devoted to them.

TOP 3 2022 NFL TOTAL TEAM SALARIES

$203 million

Los Angeles Chargers

$200 million

Jacksonville Jaguars

$195 million

Cincinnati Bengals

HOUSTON ASTROS FAN ATTENDANCE

In 2015, the Houston Astros started to play better than they had before. They won more games. They made it to championship games. Fans bought more tickets because of this. The team uses these stats to predict future sales.

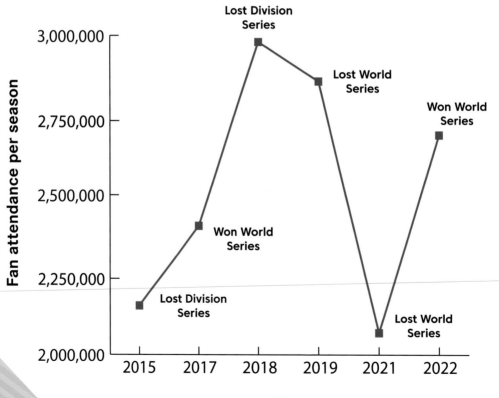

2022, Baseball-Reference.com

RECORD-BREAKING STATS

Breaking a record is a big deal. There are many kinds of records. It can be hard to keep track. Statistics is a way to keep track. It can track records in league and team histories. Some records are held for many years before they are broken. But why does it take so long to break them? Some records are statistically harder to break.

NHL: THEY SHOOT, THEY SCORE

80%

Highest shootout scoring percentage held by Petteri Nummelin

Shootout Scoring Percentage:
# of goals made / # of shots taken

Highest face-off winning percentage held by Yanic Perreault

62.86%

Face-off Win Percentage:
# of face-offs won / # of face-offs taken

HOCKEY TERMS:

shootout: **when a game ends in a tie and each team is given the chance to take three shots**

face-off: **when the referee drops the puck between two players, the first player to get possession of the puck wins the face-off**

WAYNE GRETZKY: THE GREAT ONE

17.6%

WAYNE GRETZKY'S CAREER SHOOTING PERCENTAGE

Shooting Percentage:
goals made / number of shots taken

41%

Percent by which he broke the previous record

1986

Year he set all-time single-season points record

MLB RECORDS

.864%
Highest stolen base percentage (SB%) – Carlos Beltrán

Stolen Base Percentage:
# of steals / # of attempts

.6094%
Highest single-season on-base percentage (OBP) – Barry Bonds

.426%
Highest single-season batting average (BA) – Nap Lajoie

.9847%
Highest career in-field fielding percentage (FP) – Omar Vizquel

1.82
Lowest earned run average (ERA) – Ed Walsh

Fielding Percentage:
(put outs + assists) / (put outs + assists + errors)

2022, ESPN

FOOTBALL RECORDS

105.8
Highest passing rating held by Patrick Mahomes
Passing Rating: (# of completions / attempts – .3) x 5

67.8%
Highest completion percentage held by Deshaun Watson
Completion Percentage:
(% of passes thrown for completions – 30) x .05

47.6
Highest yards per punt tied between Michael Dickson
and Shane Lechler
Yards per punt (sometimes known as punt yardage):
total yards per punt / total # of punts

FOOTBALL TERMS:

completion: when a receiver catches a forward pass thrown by the quarterback without the ball touching the ground

punt: a kick performed by dropping the ball from the hands and then kicking the ball before it hits the ground

17

THE FUTURE OF SPORTS STATS

Some people really like sports statistics and analytics. So they do it for a living! Sports analytics is now a global **industry.** It might be worth up to $22 billion by 2030. There are many jobs a person could have. They could be sports statisticians or data analysts. They could be talent scouts. Talent scouts go to high school and college games to find good players. People who want to have these careers study math or statistics in college.

COLLEGE MAJORS OF SPORTS STATISTICIANS

SKILLS NEEDED FOR SPORTS STATISTICIANS

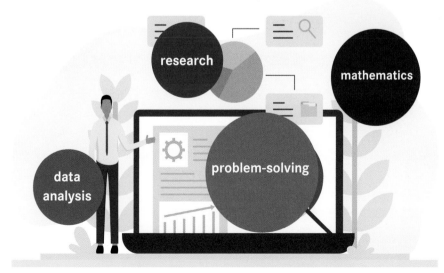

WORLDWIDE GROWTH OF SPORTS ANALYTICS

Growth Rates

- High
- Medium
- Low
- No Info

Drivers of Growth

American Football

Baseball

Basketball

Cricket

Hockey

Soccer

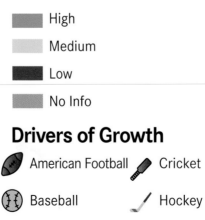

ACTIVITY

Predict the Winner

Want to practice your statistical skills? Put them to the test by creating your own March Madness bracket!

Materials Needed

• Computer access   • Paper   • Writing utensil

1. Research statistics from the previous college basketball season. Look at the team stats and compare them. Be sure to keep the honor system. Don't peek at which teams made it to the finals!

2. Draw a blank bracket. See the example below. Then use your stat research to fill it in and make your predictions.

3. Research the outcome of March Madness for that season. Did your stat research help you predict correctly?

GAME 1

Team A

Winner of GAME 1

Team B

GAME 3

Team C

Winner of GAME 3

Winner of GAME 2

Team D

GAME 2

FIND OUT MORE

Books

Berglund, Bruce R. *Football GOATs: The Greatest Athletes of All Time.* North Mankato, MN: Capstone Press, 2022.

Buckley, James, Jr. *It's a Numbers Game: Baseball.* Washington, DC: National Geographic Kids, 2021.

Swanson, Jennifer. *The Secret Science of Sports: The Math, Physics, and Mechanical Engineering Behind Every Grand Slam, Triple Axel, and Penalty Kick.* New York: Black Dog & Leventhal, 2021.

Online Resources to Explore with an Adult

Sports Illustrated Kids

Sports Reference

Bibliography

Abee, Jerrod. "The Slow Growth of Data Analytics in the Football." Samford University. January 6, 2022.

Kashyap, Hitesh. "A Primer on Sports Analytics: A New Dimension of Sports." *Analytics India Magazine*. August 5, 2021.

Steinberg, Leigh. "Changing the Game: The Rise of Sports Analytics." *Forbes*. August 18, 2015.

Thompson, Derek. "The Most Amazing Statistical Achievement in U.S. Sports History." *The Atlantic*. January 21, 2022.

GLOSSARY

analytics (an-uh-LIH-tiks) the careful study of information in order to find patterns and come to conclusions

data (DAY-tuh) numbers and facts about a certain subject that are collected and studied

evaluate (ee-VAL-yoo-ate) to study in order to determine significance, worth, or condition

industry (IN-duh-stree) a group of businesses that provide a similar service

league (LEEG) an organized group of sports teams that play against each other

metric (MEH-trick) a type of measurement

player tracking (PLAY-ur TRAK-ing) technology used to collect information about sports players and their performance

predictions (pruh-DIK-shuns) statements about what might happen in the future

revenue (REH-vuh-noo) money that is made by a business or group

statistics (stuh-TISS-tikz) a branch of math that studies information in order to draw conclusions

INDEX